ENGLISCH FÜR KINDER

READ ENGLISH WITH ZIGZAG -1, 2 and 3

ISBN: 978-1-914911-64-4

www.zigzagenglish.co.uk

www.zigzagenglish.co.uk – BOOKS FOR ENGLISH LEARNERS

OUR BOOKS FOR CHILDREN

Our bilingual picture books for younger children. *Funny stories in simple, useful everyday English, with colour photos.*
English with Tony -1- Tony moves house
English with Tony -2- Tony is happy
English with Tony -3- Tony's Christmas
English with Tony -4- Tony's holiday
My best friend

Our coursebook for beginners *(age 7 to 11)*
English for Children - 1st Coursebook *(Essential vocabulary and grammar for beginners)*

Our dialogue books for beginners *(age 7 to 11).*
I Speak English Too! - 1
I Speak English Too! - 2

Our series of reading and comprehension books for beginners *(age 7 to 11).*
Read English with Zigzag - 1
Read English with Zigzag - 2
Read English with Zigzag - 3
Audiobook at Audible.com

Our vocabulary book with photos, word puzzles and more *(age 7+)*
300+ mots en anglais / 300+ englische Wörter / 300+ palabras en inglés / 300+ parole inglesi

The Learn English Activity Book for Children *(A1 - A2, elementary).* *(Recommended for children in early secondary school.)*

Our series of reading and comprehension books for children at elementary level *(A1 - A2) (recommended for ages 10 to 13). With lots of language activities.*
Read English with Ben - 1
Read English with Ben - 2
Read English with Ben - 3

Our YOU DECIDE adventure book with 1 beginning and 19 endings. *A2 (11+)* Your Bilingual Fairy Tale Adventure

Our series of reading and discussion books about a family with superpowers *(with writing tasks) for children at secondary school, A2 - B1*
I Live in a Castle – Book 1 – My Superpower
I Live in a Castle – Book 2 – The New Me

The Speak English, Read English, Write English Activity Books – *3 books from A1 to B2, for older children and adults.*

Our non-fiction book with language activities
Learn English with Fun Facts! – A2 - B2

English Dialogues for Teenagers – for ages 11 to 17, A2 - B2

OUR BOOKS FOR ADULTS

Our 3 Grammar books with grammar-focused dialogues
Learn English Grammar through Conversation – A1, A2 and B1

Our Dialogue books for adults *(with vocabulary lists and comprehension questions). Audiobooks are available for some of these books – at Audible.com.*
50 very Easy Everyday English Dialogues (A2)
50 Easy Everyday English Dialogues (A2 - B1)
50 Intermediate Everyday English Dialogues (B1 - B2)
50 more Intermediate Everyday English Dialogues (B1 - B2)
40 Advanced Everyday English Dialogues (B2 - C1)
40 Intermediate Business English Dialogues (B1 - B2)
40 Advanced Business English Dialogues (B2 - C1)

Our activity books for adults and older children
The Speak English, Read English, Write English Activity Books – 3 books, for A1 - A2, A2 - B1 and B1 - B2.

Our non-fiction book with language activities
Learn English with Fun Facts! – A2 - B2

Contents

Die Ziele dieser Buchreihe sind: ... 6
Wie Sie diese Buchreihe verwenden können: ... 6
Was noch? Wie geht es weiter? ... 6
READ ENGLISH WITH ZIGZAG -1 ... 7
1 I'm Zigzag ... 8
2 Poppy ... 10
3 How many animals do you know? ... 12
4 Pam's a dog ... 13
5 Do you have a pet? ... 15
6 It's my sofa ... 17
7 Adam's hungry ... 18
8 I don't want to eat cat food ... 19
9 Poppy goes to school ... 21
10 Where's my toy? ... 23
11 School ... 25
12 It's not my fault ... 27
13 At the doctor's ... 28
14 I'm sorry ... 29
15 Birthday party ... 30
16 Too many boys and girls ... 33
17 Party games ... 34
18 A very small house ... 36
19 A weekend at the seaside ... 38
20 The Boss ... 40
21 Where are they? ... 41
22 I want to... ... 42
Word Search ... 44
Antworten ... 45
READ ENGLISH WITH ZIGZAG -2 ... 47
1 I'm a tiger, remember? ... 48
2 What time is it? ... 51
3 A million bugs ... 52
4 How many animals are there? ... 54
5 Where is Poppy? ... 55
6 School uniform ... 57
7 I have an idea ... 58
8 School project ... 59
9 Be quiet ... 61
10 A quarter of an hour ... 62
11 I'm not scared ... 64
12 Picnic ... 65
13 A new plan ... 68

14 Book bag 69
15 Let me out! 71
16 Stripes and spots 72
17 YOWL! 73
18 Something strange 75
19 Not funny 76
20 The Headteacher 77
21 An exciting day 78
22 Sixty-one dogs and one spider 79
Word Search 80
Antworten: 81
READ ENGLISH WITH ZIGZAG -3 83
1 I'm not a cat 84
2 One or two things you need to know 85
3 Dogs are better than cats 86
4 Big, bigger, biggest 87
5 A long time ago 88
6 Old enough 90
7 A very brave thing 92
8 At school 95
9 Something interesting 96
10 Goldilocks and the 3 bears 98
11 Cat in a tree 101
12 Terrible danger 103
13 Dogs can't climb trees 106
14 The school rules 108
15 The plan 110
16 Lunch 112
17 A lazy cat 114
18 Animal tracks 115
19 Bad dog! 116
Find the opposites. 119
What are the words? 119
Antworten: 120
Vielen Dank, dass Sie diese Reihe gelesen haben. 122
From: I Speak English Too! - 1 123
From: I Speak English Too! - 2 124
From: Read English with Ben - 1 125
From: The Learn English Activity Book 126
Which Zigzag book 127

Die Ziele dieser Buchreihe sind:

1. Eine unterhaltsame und lustige Lektüre zu sein.
2. Ihrem Kind das Vertrauen zu geben, Englisch zu lesen.
3. Ihrem Kind Schlüsselwörter und -sätze beizubringen. Die Bücher führen diese ein, wiederholen sie und bauen sie nach und nach auf, um das Verständnis Ihres Kindes für die englische Sprache zu erweitern.
4. Ihrem Kind auf einfache Weise die Grundlagen in englischer Grammatik beizubringen.

Wie Sie diese Buchreihe verwenden können:

1. Vielleicht kann Ihr Kind die Bücher schon ohne Hilfe lesen. Das ist großartig! Aber wenn Sie Englisch sprechen, können Sie ihm bei der Aussprache helfen, indem Sie es ermutigen, Ihnen einige Kapitel laut vorzulesen. **Die Bücher 1 und 2 sind auch als Hörbuch erhältlich.**
2. In jedem Buch gibt es Vokabellisten, die Sie verwenden können, um Ihrem Kind beim Lernen der neuen Wörter zu helfen.
3. Es gibt Verständnisfragen, mit Antworten am Ende jedes Buches. Sie können natürlich weitere Fragen hinzufügen und Gespräche über die Geschichte führen.
4. Es gibt weitere sprachliche Aktivitäten, die Ihrem Kind beim Erlernen von Wortschatz und Grammatik helfen.

Was noch? Wie geht es weiter?

1. Unsere Reihe mit einfachen Dialogen - **I Speak English Too!** - ist für Eltern gedacht, die ihrem Kind helfen wollen, Englisch zu sprechen. Sie ist ideal für Eltern und Kind, oder für zwei Kinder die gemeinsam lesen und sprechen möchten. Buch 1 beginnt mit den Grundlagen, indem es Schlüsselwörter und -sätze einführt und dann vertieft, sodass Ihr Kind schnelle Fortschritte macht. Schon nach wenigen Lektionen wird Ihr Kind kleine Dialoge auf Englisch mit Ihnen führen können.
2. Das Lesen von Büchern auf Englisch - egal wie einfach sie sind - macht einen großen Unterschied. Wir empfehlen auch, einfache Fernsehserien für Kinder anzuschauen. Auch wenn sie für englische Muttersprachler konzipiert sind, die etwas jünger sind als Ihr Kind. Auch Hörbücher eignen sich hervorragend, vor allem kurz vor dem Schlafengehen (das hilft dem Kind, die neue Sprache zu beizubehalten). Erwarten Sie nicht, dass Ihr Kind alles sofort versteht - Hörbücher können immer wieder angehört werden, und Ihr Kind wird jedes Mal mehr verstehen.

READ ENGLISH WITH ZIGZAG -1

Early morning at Zigzag's house

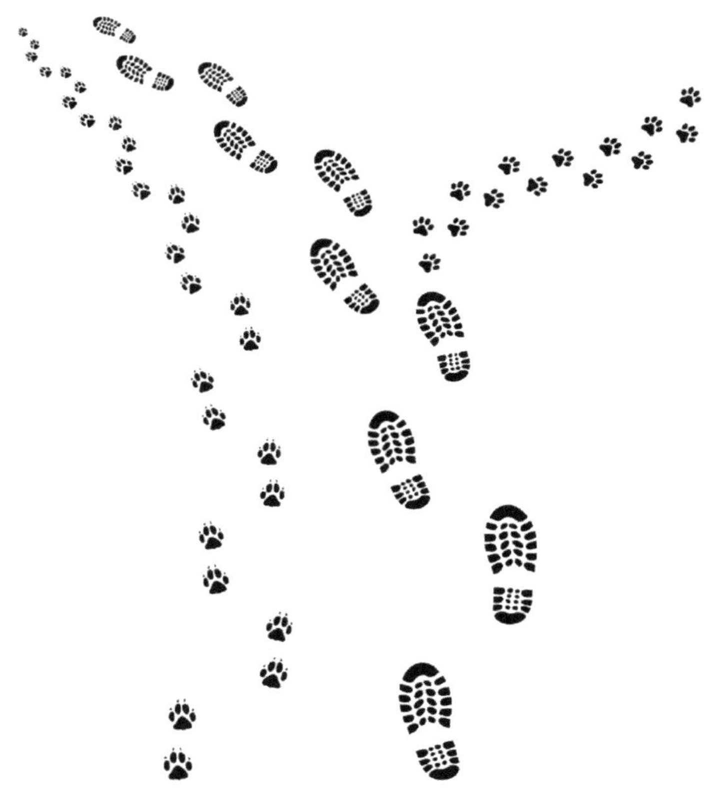

1 I'm Zigzag

Hello! My name's Zigzag. Yes, Zigzag. My name's Zigzag.

I'm six. And I'm a tiger. I'm not a cat. No, I'm not a big cat. I'm a tiger. I'm a small tiger.

What's your name? Are you a tiger? No? Are you a boy? Are you a girl? Are you big or small?

How old are you? Are you eight or nine? Or ten or eleven? I'm six.

I like big boys and girls. And I like small girls and boys.

I like **chicken** and **cheese**. And I like **cat food**. But I'm not a cat. No, I'm not. I'm a tiger.

I'm **busy today**. I'm very busy. I'm very, very busy. Are you busy?

I have to go now, because I'm busy. Can I see you **tomorrow**? Please? Please, please, please, please, please? Yes? Thank you!

Goodbye! See you tomorrow!

Vocabulary

• chicken	Huhn
• cheese	Käse
• cat food	Katzenfutter
• busy	beschäftigt
• today	heute
• tomorrow	morgen

2 Poppy

Poppy is eight. She lives in a nice house in Cambridge. Cambridge is a small **city** in England.

Poppy **lives** with her mum and dad. She has a **little** brother. His name is Adam. He's four. She doesn't have any sisters. But she has two pets – a dog and a cat.

Her cat is called Zigzag. He's **really** big. He **looks like** a little tiger. Her dog is called Pam. She's **quite** big too. She's black and white.

Poppy likes playing with her cat and her dog. And she likes playing with her friends, **too**.

Questions:

1. *Where does Poppy live?*
2. *How old is Adam?*
3. *How many pets does Poppy have?*

Vocabulary

- city — Stadt
- to live — leben
- little — klein
- really — wirklich
- to look like — aussehen wie
- quite — ziemlich
- too — auch

3 How many animals do you know?

Where is the: hamster, butterfly, spider, rabbit, snail, fish, rat, bird and snake?

4 Pam's a dog

Hello! Hello everyone! I'm Zigzag. My name's Zigzag. What's your name? Is your name Anne? No? Is it Mark? No? What IS your name? How old are you? I'm six!

This is my friend. This is my friend Pam. Pam is a dog. I'm a tiger, **but** Pam's a dog. I'm a small tiger, and Pam is a big dog. I AM NOT A CAT!

I like Pam. I don't like dogs, but I like Pam. Pam is a good dog.

Do you like dogs? Do you like dogs and tigers? Or do you like snakes and spiders?

I'm very **hungry**. I want to **eat** cat food. Pam is hungry too. Pam wants to eat dog food. Cat food is **nice**, but dog food is **horrible**. **Yuck**!

Vocabulary

• but	aber
• hungry	hungrig
• to eat	essen
• nice	gut
• horrible	furchtbar
• yuck	igitt

5 Do you have a pet?

Do you have a hamster or a rabbit? A fish or a bird? A rat or a snake?

Or do you have a cat or a dog? Which is **better**? You **choose**!

CAT or DOG?

Easy to look after?

Friendly?

Intelligent?

Fun?

Funny?

Independent?

Cute?

Beautiful?

Vocabulary

• pet	Haustier
• better	besser
• to choose	wählen
• easy	leicht
• to look after	pflegen
• friendly	freundlich
• fun	Spaß
• funny	lustig
• independent	unabhängig
• cute	süß
• beautiful	schön

6 It's my sofa

Hello! How are you? How are you today? Are you okay? I'm fine. Pam's fine too.

This is my house. My house is big. My house is **lovely**. Do you like my house?

This is my sofa. My sofa is very **comfortable**. I like my sofa. Pam likes my sofa too. But it's MY sofa! Go away, Pam!

This is my **kitchen**. This is my **fridge**. This is my cat food in the fridge.

I'm hungry. I want my cat food!

This is Poppy. Poppy, **give** me my cat food! Please, Poppy!

Thank you!

Vocabulary

- lovely — schön
- comfortable — bequem
- kitchen — Küche
- fridge — Kühlschrank
- to give — geben

7 Adam's hungry

Adam's hungry. He wants to eat:

Ice cream, crisps, biscuits, a doughnut, chocolate and sweets.

His mum wants him to eat:

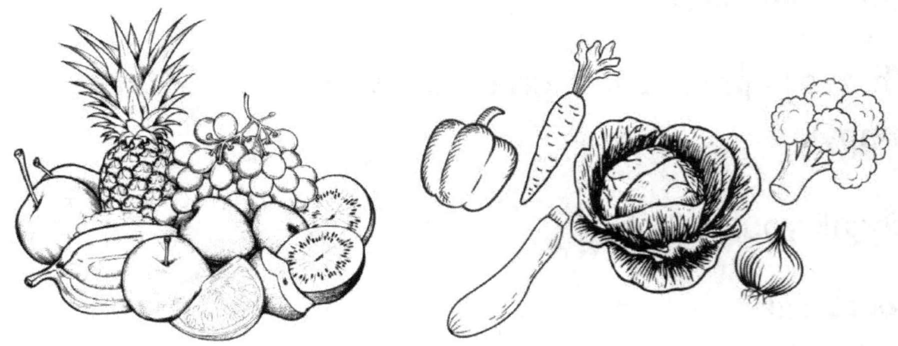

Fruit and vegetables!

Are you hungry? What do *you* want to eat?

8 I don't want to eat cat food

Hello! How are you? I'm okay today. I'm fine.

But I'm hungry. I want to eat **something**. I don't want to eat cat food. And I don't want to eat dog food. Dog food is horrible - yuck!

I want to eat... a spider! I like spiders. I like eating spiders. I like eating big, black spiders! Do you like eating spiders?

Is there a spider in the fridge? No, there's not. Is there a spider in the **garden**? Let's **look for** a spider.

Is this a spider? No, it's not a spider. It's a snail. It's a small snail. What colour is it? It's brown and white. I don't like snails.

Is this a spider? No, it's not. It's a butterfly. It's a beautiful butterfly. What colour is it? It's red, yellow and blue. I like butterflies. Butterflies are nice. They're **pretty**. But I don't like eating butterflies.

I want to eat a spider!

Vocabulary

- something etwas
- garden Garten
- to look for suchen
- pretty hübsch

9 Poppy goes to school

Poppy goes to school **every day**. No, not every day. Poppy goes to school on Monday, Tuesday, Wednesday, Thursday and Friday.

Adam doesn't go to school. He's too small to go to school. But he goes to **nursery**. Poppy likes going to school, but Adam doesn't like going to nursery. He wants to **stay** at home. He wants to play with the dog in the garden.

Poppy doesn't go to school on Saturday or Sunday. At the **weekend**, Poppy stays at home and plays with her little brother. Sometimes she goes to the park. Sometimes she goes to a friend's house.

Poppy has a **best friend**. She's called Jessica. Jessica is a beautiful name!

Questions:

1. *Does Adam go to school?*
2. *When doesn't Poppy go to school?*
3. *Where does Poppy go at the weekend?*

Vocabulary

- every day — jeden Tag
- nursery — Kindergarten
- to stay — bleiben
- weekend — Wochenende
- best friend — bester Freund

10 Where's my toy?

Hi! Is that you? Is that you **again**? It's nice to see you!

I feel **great**. I'm not hungry. I'm not hungry now. I don't want any cat food. I don't want **another** spider. One spider is **enough**.

Where is my **toy**? I want to play with it.

Is it **on** the **table**? No, it's not.

Is it **under** the sofa? No, it's not.

Is it **behind** the **armchair**? No, it's not.

Where is it? Oh, there it is. It's **next to** the television.

Pam, do you want to play with me? No, she doesn't want to play.

Poppy, do you want to play with me? No, she doesn't.

Adam, do you want to play? Adam? Where are you?

Yes! Yes! Adam wants to play. He wants to play with me! I love you, Adam!

Vocabulary

- again wieder
- great großartig
- another eine weitere
- enough genug
- toy Spielzeug
- on auf
- table Tisch
- under unter
- behind hinter
- armchair Sessel
- next to neben

11 School

Poppy and Jessica **walk** to school with Jessica's mum.

Their school is quite big. There are three hundred and fifty children at the school. There are twenty-five children in Poppy's class and twenty-six children in Jessica's class. Jessica's class is bigger than Poppy's.

Poppy's teacher is called Mrs Rice. She's nice. Poppy likes her - most of the time!

Poppy likes **learning** English, but she doesn't like **maths**. Maths is fun, but Poppy doesn't like it. She's bad at maths, but she's very good at English. Poppy likes **break times** best. Sometimes Poppy and her friends play football. Sometimes they **chat**.

On Thursdays, Poppy takes her **swimming things** to school. All the children in her class go swimming at the big **swimming pool** near their school. Everyone loves swimming. Thursday is the best day of the week.

Questions:

1. *Does Poppy go to school **by car**?*
2. *How big is Poppy's school?*
3. *Does Poppy like maths lessons best?*

Vocabulary

- to walk — zu Fuß gehen
- to learn — lernen
- maths — Mathe
- break time — Pause
- to chat — plaudern
- swimming things — Badesachen
- swimming pool — Schwimmbad
- by car — mit dem Auto

12 It's not my fault

Oh dear. **I'm sorry**. I'm really sorry, Adam.

Does it hurt, Adam?

I'm sorry. But **it's not my fault**. It's really not my fault, is it Adam? It's your fault, isn't it Adam?

Adam is **sad.** Adam has to go to the **doctor's**.

But I want to play. Where's my toy now? Poppy? Do you want to play with me?

Please play with me Poppy! Why not? Why are you **angry**? Why are you angry with me?

I'm sad now. I'm **tired**. I'm hungry. I'm really hungry. I want my cat food!

Vocabulary

• I'm sorry	es tut mir leid
• does it hurt?	tut es weh?
• it's not my fault	es ist nicht meine Schuld
• sad	traurig
• doctor	Arzt
• angry	wütend
• tired	müde

13 At the doctor's

Adam has to go to the doctor's today. Poppy goes with him.

The doctor looks at Adam's hand. His **left** hand. There's a **scratch** on his hand.

"Is there a cat at home?" asks the doctor.

"Yes", says Adam. "I like the cat, but he doesn't like me!"

The doctor puts a **plaster** on Adam's hand. "It's not a bad scratch," he says. "But be **careful** when you play with that cat. Maybe it's really a tiger?"

Questions:

1. ***Who** goes to the doctor's with Adam?*
2. *Is there a scratch on Adam's **right** hand?*
3. *What does the doctor put on Adam's hand?*

Vocabulary

- left — links
- scratch — Kratzer
- plaster — Pflaster
- careful — vorsichtig
- who — wer
- right — rechts

14 I'm sorry

Hello! How are you? Are you okay?

I'm fine. But Adam's not fine. **Poor** Adam.

Look at Adam's hand. He has a big plaster on his hand. Does your hand hurt, Adam?

His left hand hurts, but his right hand doesn't hurt. His right hand is okay.

Adam, can you play with me? Can you play with me with your right hand? Can you?

He doesn't want to play.

Adam, this is for you. This is a **present** for you.

It's a lovely big black spider.

Because I love you, Adam. And because I'm really sorry.

Vocabulary

- poor — arm
- present — Geschenk

15 Birthday party

Poppy wants to **invite** everyone in her class to her birthday party. But her mum says no. Poppy can invite nine friends.

Poppy chooses Jessica and eight other friends. Choosing's not easy.

Poppy's birthday party is so much fun. She gets lots of presents. The best present is a toy dog that **barks.** It looks just like Pam.

The **chocolate** cake is **enormous**. Chocolate cake is Poppy's favourite.

Everyone sings Happy Birthday. **Some** of the children are very bad **singers**!

The party **games** are great. The best game is Musical **Chairs**. When the music **stops**, you have to **sit** on a chair. But there aren't enough chairs! Jessica **wins** that game.

Then there are **races** in the garden. Adam wins the **egg** and **spoon** race.

Questions:

1. *How big is the birthday cake?*
2. *What do the children have to do when the music stops?*

Vocabulary

• birthday party	Geburtstagsfeier
• to invite	einladen
• to bark	bellen
• chocolate	schokolade
• enormous	riesig
• everyone	alle
• some	einige
• singer	Sänger
• game	Spiel
• chair	Stuhl
• to stop	aufhören
• to sit	sitzen
• to win	gewinnen
• race	Rennen
• egg	Ei
• spoon	Löffel

H A P P Y B I

16 Too many boys and girls

Hi there! Is it your birthday today?

It's Poppy's birthday today. Poppy is nine today.

I don't like birthday parties. They're **noisy**. They're too noisy. There are lots of children. There are too many children.

Pam likes birthday parties. She likes noisy children. She likes eating birthday cake too.

I can't sit on my sofa. There are too many children in the living room! I can't eat my cat food. There are too many children in the kitchen! I can't look for a spider in the garden. That's **right** – there are too many boys and girls there!

Mum and Dad's bedroom is **quiet**. Their bed is quite comfortable.

See you tomorrow...

Vocabulary

- noisy laut
- right richtig
- quiet ruhig

17 Party games

This is Poppy's favourite party game. It's called Musical Statues.

Play some music. Everyone **dances**.

When the music stops, everyone has to **stand still. Completely** still.

If you **move**, you're out of the game.

Play the music again.

The winner is the **last** person left.

Adam's favourite race is the egg and spoon race.

Everyone gets a spoon and an egg.

You have to put the egg in the spoon and run with it.

If you **drop** the egg, you have to **pick it up** and put it back in the spoon.

If you use **real** eggs, this race can get very **messy**!

Vocabulary

- to dance — tanzen
- to stand still — stillstehen
- completely — ganz
- to move — sich bewegen
- last — letzte

• to drop	fallen lassen
• to pick up	aufheben
• real	echt
• messy	chaotisch

18 A very small house

Look at this. It's a house. But it's very, very small.

I don't **understand**. Do you understand?

Who lives in this house? Very, very small **people**?

Where are the small people?

Are they **hiding**? Are they hiding in the yellow toy **box**? Are they hiding under the purple armchair? Are they hiding behind the white **bookcase**?

Is there a very small dog too? And a very small tiger?

I don't understand!

Vocabulary

- to understand — verstehen
- people — Menschen
- to hide — sich verstecken
- box — Kiste
- bookcase — Bücherregal

19 A weekend at the seaside

It's **summer** now. It's hot. It's too hot.

Poppy's **excited**. The family is going **away** for the weekend. They're going to a hotel by the sea.

Poppy packs her swimming things - her green **swimming costume** and her **towel**. Adam packs his red **plastic bucket**.

Pam is going to the seaside too. She's very **happy**. She takes her ball.

Adam puts Zigzag's cat toy in the car.

"Zigzag is a cat!" says Mum. "He can't come!"

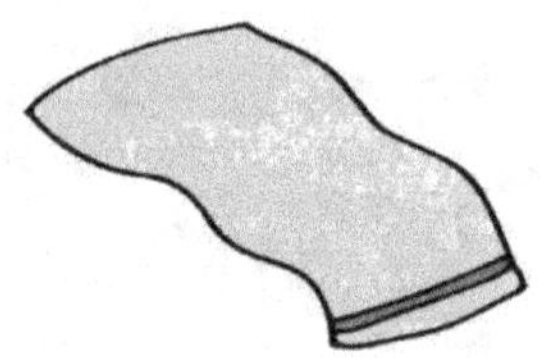

Questions:

1. *Is Poppy going to the mountains?*
2. *What does Pam take with her?*
3. *Why can't Zigzag come?*

Vocabulary

• sea / seaside	Meer
• summer	Sommer
• excited	aufgerecht
• away	weg
• swimming costume	Badeanzug
• towel	Handtuch
• plastic	aus Plastik
• bucket	Eimer
• happy	glücklich

20 The Boss

Hello. Is that you again? I want to tell you a **secret**.

Today is an **important** day.

Today, Mum and Dad and Poppy and Adam and Pam aren't here.

Tomorrow's an important day too. Because tomorrow, Pam and Adam and Poppy and Dad and Mum aren't here.

But I'm here. I'm in the house. Today and tomorrow, this is MY house. I AM THE BOSS.

And this is what I want to do...

Vocabulary

• boss	Chef
• secret	Geheimnis
• important	wichtig

21 Where are they?

in front of? in?

between? next to?

behind? on?

under?

22 I want to…

I want to:

Eat all the cat food.

Chase birds in the garden.

Scratch Dad's **special** chair.

Lick the little people in the **doll's house**.

Run up and down the **stairs** ten times.

Pull the children's **pictures off** the fridge.

Bite the **next door neighbour**.

Drink water from the toilet.

Go to sleep in Mum and Dad's bed.

PURRRRRRR… That was so much fun.

Vocabulary

- to chase — jagen
- special — besondere
- to lick — lecken
- doll's house — Puppenhaus
- stairs — Treppe
- to pull off — abreißen
- picture — Bild
- to bite — beißen
- next door neighbour — Nachbar von nebenan
- to drink — trinken
- to go to sleep — schlafen gehen

Word Search

Z	U	O	I	H	X	V	F	P	X	I	L	D	N	H
Y	D	H	Y	C	E	N	I	U	E	B	H	W	E	G
Z	U	N	D	E	R	S	T	A	N	D	A	W	I	A
G	A	M	E	N	F	B	G	Q	K	S	E	Z	G	R
F	J	F	U	I	A	T	L	D	A	L	N	P	H	D
C	L	P	B	C	H	O	C	O	L	A	T	E	B	E
X	Q	Z	K	G	Z	M	F	S	A	V	E	O	O	N
S	T	A	I	R	S	O	R	O	S	K	C	P	U	K
X	R	N	L	C	Z	R	I	F	W	U	I	L	R	O
M	D	Q	D	V	O	R	D	A	M	U	B	E	Q	Z
J	Z	K	H	Y	Z	O	G	E	O	A	B	X	X	A
G	J	Y	C	Z	M	W	E	S	H	P	C	N	G	Q
V	F	G	R	Y	S	I	M	L	N	R	C	D	E	Z
S	F	H	M	O	E	F	Q	X	L	Q	K	U	O	X
S	U	W	X	B	A	L	O	V	E	L	Y	H	D	Z

- It's summer. It's hot. I want to swim in the **s-a**.
- My **n-ighb-ur** has a **l-v-ly g-rd-n**.
- Why is the in the **fr-d-e**? Because it's hot today.
- Zigzag runs up and down the **st-ir-** all day.
- I don't **und-rst-nd** how to play the **ga-e** of Musical Chairs.
- There are 2 **peo-le** on my **s-f-**! Get off, it's MY **s-f-**!
- What do you want to do **t-m-rr-w**, Zigzag? I want to eat all the cat food!

Antworten

2

1. She lives in Cambridge in England.
2. He's four.
3. She has two pets.

3

snail, butterfly, fish, rat, spider, snake, hamster, bird, rabbit

9

1. No, he doesn't. He goes to nursery.
2. At the weekend (on Saturday and Sunday).
3. She goes to the park or to a friend's house.

11

1. No, she doesn't. She walks to school.
2. It's quite big.
3. No, she doesn't. She likes break times best.

13

1. Poppy does. Poppy goes with him.
2. No, there's not. There's a scratch on his left hand.
3. The doctor puts a plaster on Adam's hand.

15

1. It's enormous.
2. They have to sit on a chair.

19

1. No, she's not. She's going to the seaside.
2. She takes her ball with her.
3. Because he's a cat.

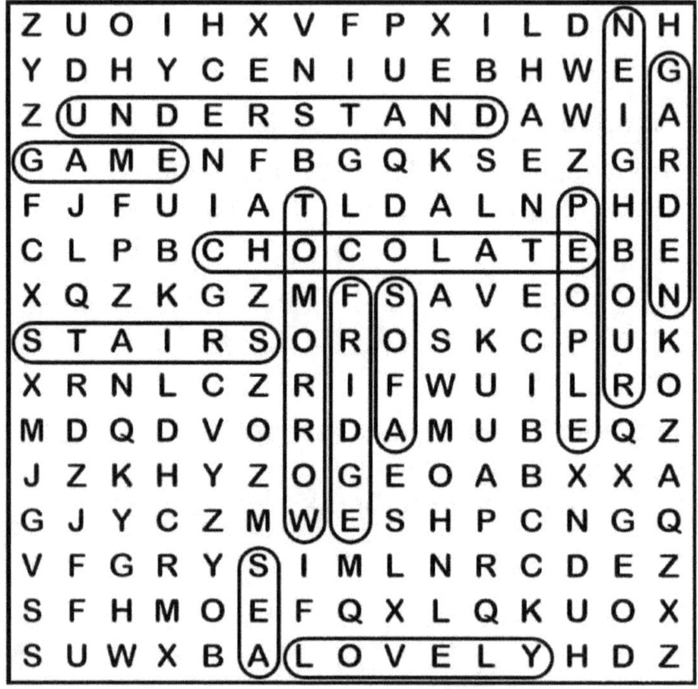

Cat or tiger?

1 I'm a tiger, remember?

Hello! I'm Zigzag. My name's Zigzag, and I'm a tiger. Yes, I'm a tiger.

No, I'm not a cat. I'm a tiger, remember?

Who are you? Are you a friend? I think you're my friend. Are you?

I live in this lovely house with my best friend, Pam. She's a dog, but I like her a lot. I'm big, but Pam is bigger. She's a very big, black and white dog.

Adam and Poppy live in my house too. They're not tigers or dogs, but they're okay. I quite like them. Sometimes they play with me. And sometimes they give me food.

What time is it? Oh! It's **dinner** time!

Poppy - WHERE'S MY CAT FOOD? GIVE ME MY CAT FOOD!

Vocabulary

- to remember erinnern
- dinner Abendessen

2 What time is it?

It's half past twelve.
It's 12:30.

It's seven o'clock in the morning.
It's 7:00 AM.

It's ten to six.
It's 5:50.

It's five past five in the afternoon.
It's 5:05 PM.

It's a quarter to four.
It's 3:45.

3 A million bugs

Hello again! Today, I want to **show** you my garden. Pam wants to show you the garden too. But it's not Pam's garden, it's my garden. Can Pam come too? Yes, she can come if she wants.

My garden has two **trees**. My garden has lots of **flowers**. But the best thing about my garden is the **bugs**. How many bugs are there in my garden? There are a million bugs!

What's my favourite bug? Can you **guess**? I think you can.

I like **bees** and butterflies. But I love spiders. Butterflies are beautiful and bees are intelligent. But spiders are **delicious**.

Vocabulary

- to show — zeigen
- tree — Baum
- flower — Blume
- bug — Wanze, Insekt
- bee — Biene
- delicious — köstlich

4 How many animals are there?

There are three animals.

How many people are there?

There is one person.

How many children are there?
There's one child.

5 Where is Poppy?

Hi there!

Can I **ask you a question**?

Where is Poppy? Why isn't she here? Where does she go every day?

Is she hiding in the house?

Is she outside, in the garden?

Do you know where she is?

I'm looking for Poppy. I'm looking for her **downstairs**, in the living-room and the kitchen. And I'm looking for her upstairs, in the bedrooms and the bathroom.

I'm looking for her **inside**, and I'm looking for her outside.

But I can't find her. Why not? Please **help** me find her!

Vocabulary

- to ask a question	eine Frage stellen
- downstairs	unten
- inside	drinnen
- to help	helfen

6 School uniform

It's Monday today and it's a quarter to nine. So Poppy's walking to school with her school friend Jessica and with Jessica's mum.

What does Jessica look like? Does she look like Poppy? No, she doesn't. Poppy has **long** brown hair and brown eyes. But Jessica has **short fair** hair and blue eyes. She's taller than Poppy.

In England, children have to wear **school uniform**. Poppy and Jessica's uniform is black **trousers** and a red top.

The girls are a bit **late** to school today. They have to run. They get to school at 9 o'clock. **Just in time.**

Questions:

1. Who is shorter, Jessica or Poppy?
2. Why do the children have to run?
3. Why are they **wearing the same** clothes?

Vocabulary:

• long	lang
• short	kurz
• fair	blond
• school uniform	Schuluniform
• trousers	Hose
• late	spät
• just in time	gerade noch rechtzeitig
• to wear	tragen
• same	gleiche

7 I have an idea

Hello everybody!

I have a problem. I **STILL** can't find Poppy.

She's not in the house - upstairs or downstairs. And she's not in the garden.

I don't know where she is. You don't know where she is. Pam doesn't know where she is.

Nobody knows where she is!

Luckily, I have an idea.

Do you want to know what my idea is?

Guess!

Vocabulary:

- idea   Idee
- still   noch
- luckily   zum Glück

8 School project

Poppy is doing a project at school. She has to ask all the children in her class about their pets. She has to **find out** what her class's favourite pet is.

Poppy **draws** a **graph**:

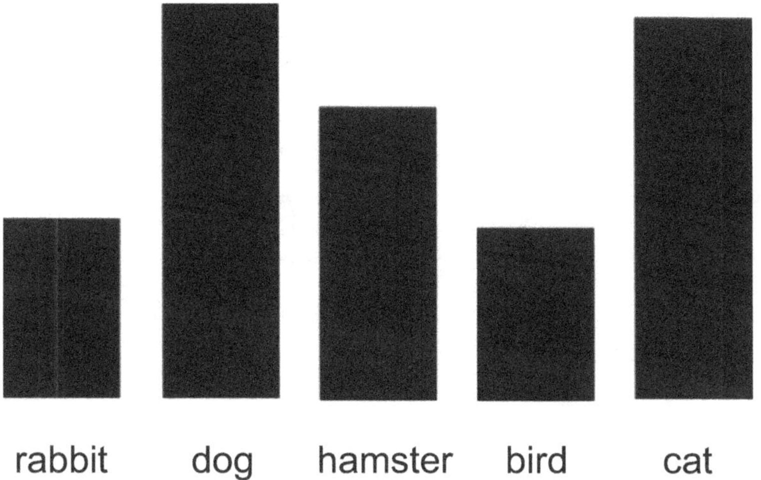

The dog is the most **popular** pet. Lots of children have dogs, but cats are very popular too. Rabbits and birds are the **least** popular pets.

Nobody has a snake or a spider. And nobody has a **lion** or a tiger.

Questions:

1. **Which** pet is the most popular?
2. Which is the least popular?
3. How many children have pet snakes?

Vocabulary:

• project	Projekt
• to find out	herausfinden
• to draw	zeichnen
• graph	Grafik
• popular	beliebt
• least	am wenigsten
• lion	Löwe
• which	welches

9 Be quiet

Shhh…

Be quiet.

Be very, very quiet.

I don't want Poppy to **hear** me. I don't want Poppy to see me. I don't want Poppy to know I'm here.

Poppy's wearing her black trousers and her red top again.

Poppy's **opening** the **door**. Poppy's going outside.

I'm going outside too! I'm going with Poppy.

Today is the day I find out where Poppy goes every day.

Do you want to come too?

Vocabulary:

- to hear — hören
- to open — öffnen
- door — Tür

10 A quarter of an hour

Poppy and Jessica are going to school again today. Walking to school takes them fifteen minutes – a **quarter** of an hour.

First they turn left. Then they turn right. Then they cross the **main road** at the **zebra crossing**.

Some children go to school by car and some go by **bike**. But most children walk to school with their mum or dad.

There are lots of children and parents **in front of** the school. They're **waiting** for the school to open. Jessica and Poppy are early for school today.

Questions:

1. How long does it take Jessica and Poppy to walk to school?
2. Do all the children at their school walk to school?
3. Why are there so many people outside the school?

Vocabulary:

- quarter — Viertel
- main road — Hauptstraße
- zebra crossing — Zebrastreifen
- bike — Fahrrad
- in front of — vor [der]
- to wait — warten

11 I'm not scared

Are you there? Are you coming with me?

Be **careful**! Be careful of the cars!

Quick - **cross** the road now!

Where's Poppy? There she is. She's with Jessica.

But who are all the **other** people? There are so **many** people here. And so many cars and bikes.

Are you **scared**? Don't be scared.

I'm not scared. I'm **never** scared.

WHAT'S THAT?! IS IT A VERY BIG DOG?!

RUN!!

Vocabulary:

- careful vorsichtig
- quick schnell
- to cross überqueren
- other andere
- many viele
- to be scared Angst haben
- never nie

12 Picnic

This weekend, Poppy and Adam's family is going on a picnic by the **river**.

The picnic is delicious. There are chicken sandwiches, cheese and **ham** sandwiches, little tomatoes, **strawberries** and **lemon cake**. There's **orange juice** to drink. There's dog food for Pam.

It's a beautiful day. It's **sunny** but not too hot.

Mum and dad are tired. They go to sleep.

Poppy **reads** her book. She's reading about tigers in India. It's very **interesting**. Poppy really likes tigers.

Suddenly, she hears Adam **shouting** – "HELP!" He's **falling** into the river!

Poppy runs. But Pam runs **faster**. She **jumps** into the **water**. She helps Adam. He's **safe** now.

That was **scary**.

Well done, Pam. Good dog!

Questions:

1. Where are Poppy's family having a picnic?
2. Why do mum and dad go to sleep?
3. What happens to Adam?

Vocabulary:

- river Fluss
- ham Schinken
- strawberry Erdbeere
- lemon cake Zitronenkuchen
- orange juice Orangensaft
- sunny sonnig
- to read lesen
- interesting interessant
- suddenly plötzlich
- to shout schreien
- to fall fallen
- faster schneller
- to jump springen
- water Wasser
- safe sicher
- scary beängstigend
- well done gut gemacht

:

13 A new plan

Hello! Remember - be quiet! Shhh...

Yes, I'm trying again today.

I have a new idea. I have a new plan.

Look over there. Look at Poppy's bag. Look at her red book **bag**.

How many books are there in Poppy's bag? Is there one book in the bag? Are there two books in the bag? Or are there no books in the bag?

There are no books in the bag.

No books, but one cat.

Vocabulary:

- bag Tasche

14 Book bag

Poppy's walking to school. She walks to school every day. She walks to school on Monday, Tuesday, Wednesday, Thursday and Friday.

But today, something is different. Poppy's bag is **heavy**.

Her bag is often heavy. It's a book bag – a bag for books – and books are heavy.

But today the bag is really heavy. **Extremely** heavy.

Something else is different, too.

Today, Poppy's bag is **moving**.

Is there something in the bag? Is it a book? Or - is it something else?

Questions:

1. What kind of bag does Poppy have?
2. Why is her bag so heavy today?
3. How heavy is the bag?

Vocabulary:

• heavy	schwer
• extremely	extrem
• something else	etwas anderes
• to move	bewegen

15 Let me out!

Are you there? Can you hear me?

You can't see me, because I'm in Poppy's book bag.

It's very **uncomfortable** in here. I'm big, and the bag is small. The bag is too small for a tiger.

I'm hot and **thirsty**.

I want to get **out**.

I can't get out! I'm **stuck**! I'm stuck in this horrible bag!

I **hate** this bag. I hate it, hate it, hate it, HATE it!

Poppy! Let me out!

POPPY!!

Vocabulary:

- uncomfortable — unbequem
- thirsty — durstig
- out — raus
- to be stuck — feststecken
- to hate — hassen

16 Stripes and spots

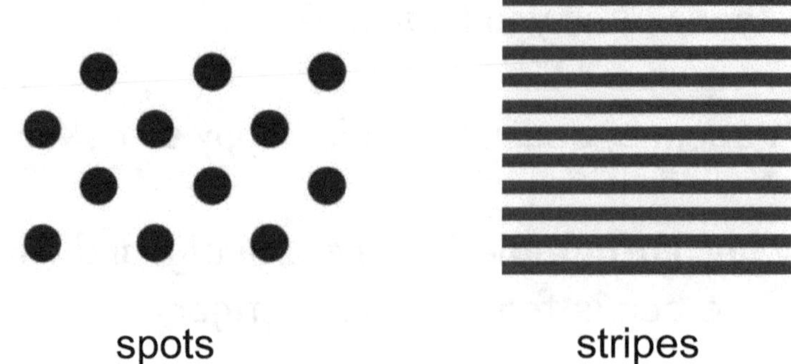

spots stripes

Who do these stripes and spots belong to?

1  2

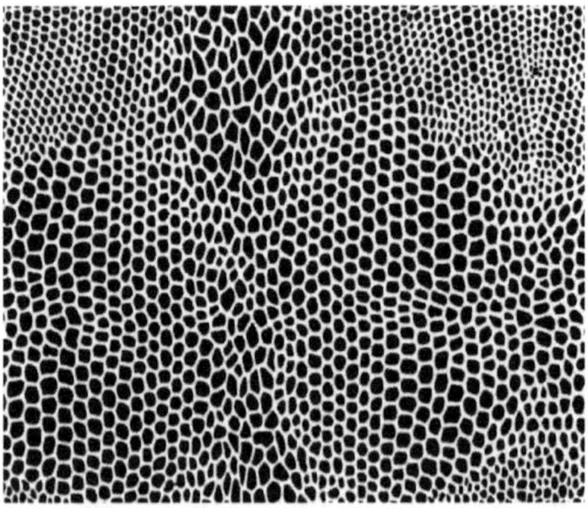

3  4

18 Something strange

Today, when Poppy and Jessica get to school, something **strange** happens.

Poppy goes into her **classroom** and says hello to her friends. The teacher, Mrs Rice, tells the children to sit down. She gives them **work** to do. Poppy needs a book. She opens her book bag.

And then…

Something jumps out of the bag. Something big. It makes a very strange noise. Then it runs **round** the classroom. It runs very fast. Three times round the room. Children are **screaming** and climbing onto chairs. Mrs Rice is shouting. "Stop it!" she shouts. "Everyone sit down! Poppy, take that cat home. Now."

Questions:

1. Why does Poppy open her book bag?
2. How many times does Zigzag run round the room?
3. What does the teacher tell Poppy to do?

Vocabulary:

• strange	seltsam
• classroom	Klassenzimmer
• work	Arbeit
• round	um
• to scream	schreien

19 Not funny

It's you again, is it? Okay.

Why are you looking at me? Are you **laughing** at me? Stop laughing. It's not funny.

Yes, I'm back home. Yes, Poppy and her mum and dad are angry with me.

Why are they angry? I don't understand. It's not my fault. It's all Poppy's fault.

I don't like Poppy. I don't like her mum and dad. I don't like this house.

I'm going outside. I want to hide from all the people. I want to hide from Pam, and I want to hide from you.

Please **leave me alone** now.

Vocabulary:

- to laugh — lachen
- to leave alone — in Ruhe lassen

20 The Headteacher

Poppy's **in trouble**. Cats aren't **allowed** in the classroom. Why was Zigzag in Poppy's bag? Poppy says it's Zigzag's fault, but the teacher doesn't **believe** her. She thinks it's Poppy's fault.

Poppy has to **talk** to the Headteacher. She **tells** her about Zigzag and the book bag. She says sorry.

The Headteacher **smiles**. The Headteacher laughs. The Headteacher has an idea.

It's a great idea. Poppy's very happy. All the children are excited.

I can't wait to tell Zigzag, thinks Poppy.

Questions:

1. Who is angry about Zigzag coming to school?
2. Who thinks it's funny?
3. What do you think the Headteacher's idea is?

Vocabulary:

- to be in trouble — Ärger haben
- allowed — erlaubt
- to believe — glauben
- to talk — reden
- to tell — erzählen
- to smile — lächeln

21 An exciting day

Hi! It's great to see you!

Today is an **exciting** day. A very exciting day. I'm so excited!

I'm going to school with Poppy today. Yes, that's right, I'm going to school with Poppy again.

This time, Poppy WANTS me to go to school with her.

I'm not going to school in Poppy's book bag. No, this time I'm going to school in my cat **basket**.

Look at me in my beautiful cat basket! Look at me, everyone!

And look at Pam – she's coming too.

There are lots of cats and dogs at school today.

Poppy – can I go to school with you every day?

Vocabulary:

- exciting aufregend
- basket Korb

22 Sixty-one dogs and one spider

Today is the day when pets can come to school.

Yes, the Headteacher's idea is that today, and only today, all the children can bring their pets to school.

There are 61 dogs. There are 53 cats. There are 17 hamsters. There are 8 rabbits. There are 5 birds. There are 3 rats. There are 2 snakes. There is 1 spider.

I hope the dogs don't chase the cats and the rabbits. I hope the cats don't eat the birds and the hamsters. I hope the rats, the snakes and the spider stay in their cages.

It's a scary day. But it's a good day too.

Can you read these numbers?

61 = sixty-one
53 = fifty-three
17 = seventeen

How about these numbers?
2782 = two thousand, seven hundred and eighty-two
90,511 = ninety thousand, five hundred and eleven

Word Search

J	F	A	F	G	H	A	D	S	W	K	D	U	E	X
Y	P	L	L	U	G	C	C	N	A	D	H	W	N	A
S	B	Q	Y	E	O	P	C	H	D	L	D	P	U	S
J	Y	R	J	S	T	P	Z	F	E	H	A	A	F	U
L	V	F	X	S	X	L	M	C	L	A	V	U	F	F
P	V	R	D	H	V	L	T	H	I	R	S	T	Y	K
S	O	I	S	U	N	G	I	O	C	V	K	A	Q	T
P	O	P	U	L	A	R	R	R	I	V	E	R	U	E
F	U	N	N	Y	G	L	E	M	O	N	C	O	F	E
H	T	P	N	I	D	X	D	D	U	N	A	E	O	E
S	S	E	Y	T	K	S	G	W	S	C	J	E	Y	H
Q	I	U	D	L	L	K	O	P	P	B	Q	E	B	V
K	D	L	L	Q	A	G	K	H	G	I	M	A	I	K
M	E	X	T	R	E	M	E	L	Y	Z	F	L	K	W
A	J	H	S	J	U	S	C	P	P	Y	O	R	E	N

- It's a hot, **su_n_** day. I want to have a picnic **o_ts_de** by the **ri_e_.** We can go swimming.
- It's too hot! Adam's **ex_r_mely t_red** and **th_r_ty**. He drinks lots of water and goes to bed.
- What are Poppy and Adam like? Poppy is **pop_l_r** – she has lots of friends. Adam is **f_n_y**. He makes me laugh!
- Do you walk to school, or do you go by **b_k_**?
- This cake is **deli_i_u_**!
- How old are you? - **Gu_ss**!

Antworten:

6

1. Poppy is shorter.
2. Because they're late to school.
3. Because they're wearing school uniform.

8

1. The dog is the most popular.
2. The bird is the least popular.
3. No children have snakes.

10

1. It takes them fifteen minutes (a quarter of an hour) to walk to school.
2. No, some go to school by car or bike.
3. Because they're waiting for the school to open.

12

1. They're having a picnic by the river.
2. Because they're tired.
3. He falls into the river.

14

1. She has a book bag.
2. Because there's a cat in it.
3. It's extremely heavy.

16

1. A zebra.
2. A dalmatian dog.
3. A snake.
4. A leopard.

18

1. Because she needs a book.
2. He runs round the room three times.
3. She tells her to take her cat home.

20

1. Poppy's teacher is angry.
2. The Headteacher thinks it's funny.

READ ENGLISH WITH ZIGZAG -3

From wolf to pet dog

1 I'm not a cat

Oh, look at all those children. Hello, children! I'm your friend! Can I **wash** your **face** for you? Is that okay? Can we go for a walk? Can I take my ball? Can you **throw** the ball for me?

What's that? What did you say?

I'm not Zigzag, no. I'm not a cat. I'm not a tiger. Do I look like a cat or a tiger?

No, I don't. I look like a dog. That's because I AM A DOG.

I'm a beautiful, big, black and white dog. I'm white with black spots. I'm a dalmatian dog.

Do you know my name? Do you remember who I am?

That's right. I'm Pam!

Vocabulary:

- to wash — waschen
- face — Gesicht
- to throw — werfen

2 One or two things you need to know

If you have a dog:

1. You have to take your dog for a walk every morning.

2. You have to take your dog for a walk every evening.

3. Do NOT **forget** to take your dog for a walk!

Vocabulary:

- to forget vergessen

3 Dogs are better than cats

I'm Pam. I'm not Zigzag, I'm Pam.

Sorry about that.

No, I'm not sorry. I'm not sorry - I'm **happy**. I'm happy, because - *guess what?* I'm **better** than Zigzag.

I'm a dog, and Zigzag is a cat. Zigzag is NOT A TIGER. He's a cat.

Dogs are better than cats. So - I'm better than Zigzag. **Right?**

I'm bigger than Zigzag. I'm nicer than Zigzag. I'm more beautiful than Zigzag. I'm more intelligent than Zigzag. I like children more than Zigzag does.

And this is my book. It's not Zigzag's book - it's mine!

Vocabulary:

- happy glücklich
- better besser
- right? oder?

4 Big, bigger, biggest

This is a small dog. It's not very big. It's the smallest dog.

This is a bigger dog. It's quite big.

This dog is even bigger. It's the biggest dog. It's really very big. It's enormous.

5 A long time ago

Some dogs are big and some dogs are small. Some dogs have long **ears** and some dogs have short **tails**. Some dogs are brown and some dogs are white with black spots **like** me.

Some dogs...

Okay, you know what I mean. All dogs are **different**.

But a very, very, very, very, very long time ago, all dogs were the same. That's right - all dogs were:

WOLVES!!

Wolves are enormous. Wolves have **sharp teeth**. Wolves are really scary. But most of all, wolves are **BRAVE**.

A long time ago, I was a wolf. Now, I'm a dog and I live in Adam and Poppy's house with Zigzag the cat.

But I'm still brave.

Vocabulary:

- a long time ago — vor langer Zeit
- ear — Ohr
- tail — Schwanz
- like — wie
- different — anders
- sharp — scharf
- tooth — Zahn
- brave — mutig

6 Old enough

Adam is four years **younger** than Poppy. When Adam was a baby, Poppy was **already** at school. When Adam **learned** to talk, Poppy learned to read. When Adam learned to walk, Poppy learned to run races.

Then Adam went to nursery with the other very small children and **painted** pictures with his hands. And Poppy started to **write stories**.

But now, **at last**, Adam's old enough to go to school with Poppy.

On his first day at school, Adam was excited. He really wanted to go to school. He didn't want to be little. He wanted to be a big boy.

He walked to school with Mum and with Poppy and her best friend Jessica. He wore his **own** school uniform – black trousers and a red top. He had his own red **book bag**. He felt **proud**. He **felt** a little bit scared.

Questions:

1. *How much older than Adam is Poppy?*
2. *How did Adam feel about starting school?*
3. *Why was his book bag red?*

Vocabulary:

- younger jünger
- already bereits
- to learn lernen

- to paint malen
- to write schreiben
- story Geschichte
- at last endlich
- own eigene
- book bag Büchertasche
- proud stolz
- to feel fühlen

7 A very brave thing

This summer, I did a very brave thing. I did the bravest thing a dog can do.

We all went for a picnic. Well, not Zigzag, because he's a cat. Cats have to stay at home.

There was a river. Mum and Dad and Poppy and I can swim. But Adam can't swim. He's too young.

Adam was in **danger**. Mum and Dad and Poppy were there. But they didn't **see** the danger.

I saw the danger. I saw Adam run and fall into the water. I jumped into the water. It was **deep**. It was too deep for me.

I swam to Adam. He put his arms round my **neck**. I **pulled** him out of the water.

Everyone said "Good dog! Brave dog!"

I'm a big, strong, brave dog and I **saved** Adam.

Vocabulary:

- danger Gefahr

- to see sehen
- deep tief
- neck Hals
- to pull ziehen
- to save retten

8 At school

At school, there were so many children. There were hundreds of them. **Nearly all** of them were older and bigger than Adam. Because it was Adam's first day, Mum was there. She took a photo of Adam in front of the school. And then she went into the classroom with Adam. Adam wanted Mum to stay with him. He started to **cry**. But Mum said goodbye, and she **left**.

Adam looked at all the other boys and girls in his class. There were lots and lots of them. He **only** knew one of them. Billy, from nursery. Adam didn't like Billy, and Billy didn't like Adam. "Hello, Billy," said Adam. Billy said **nothing**.

Adam sat on the **floor** with all the other children. The teacher told a story. It was the story of Goldilocks and the Three Bears.

Questions:

1. *Why did mum go into the classroom with Adam?*
2. *Was Adam happy to be at school?*
3. *Why didn't Billy talk to Adam?*

Vocabulary:

- nearly — fast
- all — alle
- to cry — weinen
- to leave — verlassen
- only — nur
- nothing — nichts
- floor — Boden

9 Something interesting

Adam went to school today. It was very quiet here without him.

Mum and dad were **out**. Poppy and Adam were at school. Only Zigzag was here. I like Zigzag, but he's **just** a cat. He doesn't understand much. He went to school with Poppy once, but I don't think he learned **anything**.

I went into the garden. I watched Zigzag **catch** a spider. I watched Zigzag eat the spider. Zigzag said it was delicious. I looked for a spider, but I couldn't find one.

Then I saw something interesting. Something very interesting. The next door neighbour's white cat was in the next door neighbour's garden.

I did a bad thing. I knew it was a bad thing, but I did it.

I **barked** at the cat - WOOF WOOF! Then I jumped over the **fence** into the next door neighbour's garden. The cat ran. I chased her. I chased her round and round the garden and up the neighbour's tree. She sat in the tree and looked at me.

Vocabulary:

- out aus
- just nur
- he didn't learn anything er hat nichts gelernt
- to catch fangen
- to bark bellen
- fence Zaun

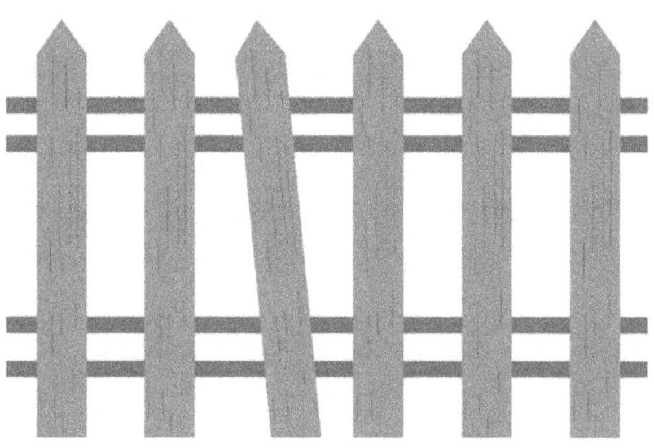

10 Goldilocks and the 3 bears

Goldilocks was a girl with gold hair (really?) who went into the **forest**, looking for some breakfast.

She found it in a bears' house (do bears live in houses?) and ate it.

Luckily for Goldilocks, the bears were out. Bears are extremely big and strong and sometimes eat little girls.

Then Goldilocks sat on a little chair and **broke** it.

She was tired, so she went upstairs to the bedroom and went to sleep on Baby Bear's bed.

When the three bears got **back** home, they were hungry. They wanted to eat their breakfast, but it was gone. Baby Bear wanted to sit on his chair, but it was broken. When they found Goldilocks on Baby Bear's bed, Father Bear wanted to eat her, but Baby Bear wanted to play with her.

Goldilocks **woke up**. She was scared. She jumped out of the window and ran home. She never went into the forest again.

Questions:

1. *Why did Goldilocks go into the forest?*
2. *Were the bears at home?*
3. *Did Baby Bear want to eat Goldilocks?*

12 Terrible danger

Adam **listened** to the story, but he didn't like it. It was scary.

The teacher showed the children a picture of Goldilocks. She was a very small girl. Then the teacher showed them a picture of the three bears. Baby Bear was quite **cute**, but Mother Bear was enormous and Father Bear was the biggest bear **ever**.

Adam knew Goldilocks was in **terrible** danger. **If** the bears came home and found Goldilocks in their house, they would **probably** eat her. If she tried to run away, they would chase her and catch her. **Then** they would eat her.

When the teacher read that Goldilocks climbed onto Baby Bear's bed and went to sleep, Adam **jumped up** and **shouted**: "Don't go to sleep, Goldilocks! **Run away**! The bears are coming!" The teacher looked at Adam and told him to sit down and be quiet.

Father Bear didn't eat Goldilocks. But he very nearly did, thought Adam.

Questions:

1. *Which bear was the biggest?*
2. *What did Baby Bear look like?*
3. *What was the most dangerous thing Goldilocks did?*

Vocabulary:

- to listen zuhören
- cute süß
- ever aller Zeiten
- terrible schrecklich
- if wenn
- probably wahrscheinlich
- then dann
- to jump up aufspringen
- to shout schreien
- to run away weglaufen

ABCDE
FGHIJK
LMNOPQ
RSTUV
WXYZ

13 Dogs can't climb trees

Do you know what I **decided** to do?

Dogs can't climb trees. That was the problem. Dogs can't climb trees, but cats can. So the white cat was in the tree, and I was under the tree. The cat was safe. Or was she?

It was **simple**, really.

Most cats are my **enemies**. But one is my friend. That's right – Zigzag is my friend, my family.

I jumped back over the fence into my garden and looked for Zigzag. He was where he **usually** is. He was on the sofa in the living room, sleeping.

I bit his tail just a little bit, to wake him up. He wasn't happy. He **hissed** at me.

I **explained** my problem with the white cat.

"Please help me, Zigzag," I said.

"Okay," said Zigzag. "But only if you **give** me what I want".

Maybe he's more intelligent than I thought.

Vocabulary:

- to decide entscheiden
- simple einfach
- most die meisten
- enemy Feind
- usually normalerweise
- to hiss zischen
- to explain erklären
- to give geben

14 The school rules

After the story, Adam's class went into the school **hall** - the biggest room in the school. All the other children in the school were already there, sitting on the floor.

The Headteacher **welcomed** the new children in Adam's class to the school. Then everyone **stood up** and sang a **song**. Adam didn't **know** what to sing, but he tried to **copy** the others.

After that, the Headteacher read the school **rules**:

1. Get to school on time.
2. Listen to the teacher.
3. Put your hand up if you want to ask a question.
4. Always **try hard**.
5. Don't **waste time**.
6. Be **kind** and polite.

Adam was **worried**. He wanted to ask a question, but he was too scared to put his hand up.

If a child broke a rule, was there a **punishment**?

Questions:

1. *What was the biggest room in the school called?*
2. *Which school rule do you think is the most important?*
3. *If you break a school rule at your school, is there a punishment?*

Vocabulary:

• hall	Saal
• to welcome	begrüßen
• to stand up	aufstehen
• song	Lied
• to know	wissen
• to copy	kopieren
• rule	Regel
• to try hard	sich anstrengen
• to waste time	Zeit verschwenden
• kind	freundlich
• worried	besorgt
• punishment	Strafe

15 The plan

This was the plan. It wasn't **difficult**. In fact, I thought it was very easy.

Zigzag is much bigger than the white cat. He just had to climb the tree and chase the white cat down to me. Simple.

But first, I had to do something for Zigzag.

Poor Zigzag. Because he's just a cat, he can't do much. He can't open the kitchen door. He can't open the fridge door. He can't take the cat food out of the fridge.

Zigzag hates waiting for dinner time. So he **often** asks me to give him his cat food. I **always** say no. Zigzag eats too much. **More** food isn't good for him.

But I really, really wanted that white cat. So, just this **once**, I opened the kitchen door and opened the fridge door. I took the cat food out of the fridge.

Zigzag ate some cat food. "I'm tired now," he said. "I want to go to sleep on my sofa".

"Oh no." I said. "Now you have to do what *I* want. Climb that tree!"

Vocabulary:

- difficult schwierig
- often oft
- always immer
- more mehr
- once einmal

16 Lunch

Adam was hungry. When he went to nursery, he had a snack at eleven o'clock every morning. Today, he had to wait **until** lunchtime at half past twelve.

He played with sand and water and balls. He painted a picture of his cat and dog. He looked at the picture books in the big **bookcase**. He tried to write his name with a **pencil**.

And at last it was lunchtime. Some children had **packed lunches** from home in beautiful lunchboxes. They ate their sandwiches outside in the **playground.** But Adam went to the big hall again. This time, it was **full** of tables and chairs. He **queued** up for his food and sat down at a table next to a boy from his class. Lunch was chicken with **mashed potato** and **peas**. With strawberry ice cream for **pudding**. It wasn't delicious, but it wasn't too bad.

After lunch, Adam and his new friend ran outside. Adam saw Poppy playing football with the **older** boys and girls. He started to **enjoy** school.

Questions:

1. *What was the most fun thing that Adam did?*
2. *What do you think of Adam's school lunch? Was it like your school lunches?*

Vocabulary:

• until	bis
• bookcase	Bücherregal
• pencil	Bleistift
• packed lunch	Lunchpaket
• playground	Schulhof
• full	voll
• to queue	anstehen
• mashed potato	Kartoffelpüree
• pea	Erbse
• older	älter
• to enjoy	Genießen

17 A lazy cat

Zigzag wasn't happy. He's a lazy cat. To be honest, he's an extremely lazy cat. He never wants to help people. He never wants to help other animals. He only thinks about himself. It's not really his fault. He's just a cat.

He walked into the garden. Very slowly. He jumped onto the garden fence. He jumped down into the neighbour's garden. He looked up at the tree. The white cat looked down at him. She stayed exactly where she was.

Then Zigzag ran at the tree. He jumped. And he fell. He fell back down. Zigzag is a big cat. He's a fat cat. I don't think he's very good at climbing trees.

Zigzag looked at me. "You ate the cat food." I said. "Now climb the tree!" Zigzag tried again. This time he **made it**. He was in the tree. But where was the white cat?

Vocabulary:

- to make it — es schaffen

18 Animal tracks

Look out for animal tracks in your garden or park. You can find them in snow or mud.

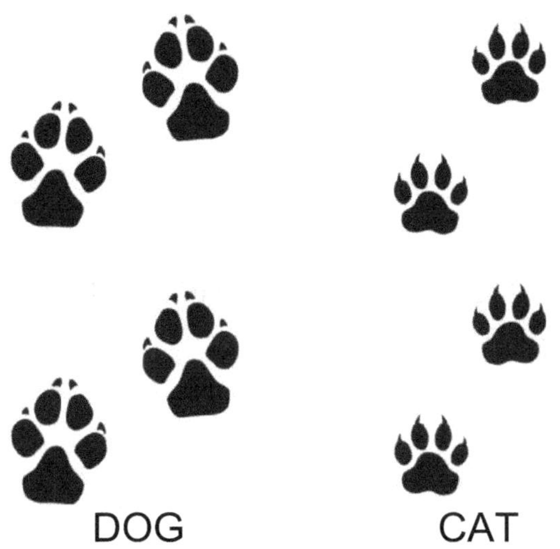

Watch out for bears – they're dangerous!

19 Bad dog!

The white cat was at the **top** of the tree. She was at the end of a thin branch.

"Go on, Zigzag! Chase that cat down!"

Zigzag slowly climbed up the tree. He climbed higher and higher. He climbed onto the white cat's branch. He was **almost** there.

CRACK!!

The branch broke. Zigzag fell down. The white cat fell down. I saw her and she saw me. She ran and I ran. I chased that cat round the garden. I chased her round the garden again. I chased her onto the **street**. I chased her down the street.

"Pam! **Stop!** Bad dog!"

Adam? Adam and Poppy and Mum? Back from school already? Where's the white cat? Oh no. She's up **another** tree. I WANT THAT CAT!

"Oh Pam", said Adam. "I had such a great time at school today."

Vocabulary:

- top Spitze
- almost fast
- street Straße
- stop! halt!
- another ein anderer

Find the opposites.

up	go
never	in
bad	different
the same	wake up
out	noisy
stop	dangerous
quiet	down
easy	good
cute	always
safe	scary
go to sleep	difficult

What are the words?

Adam is alm-st five. He's very y-ung, but he's a pol-t- child. He al-ays says thank you.

My dad says English is quite e-sy. But I'm ter-ibl- at it!

Your English is b-t-er than my English.

Please read me the -tor- of Goldilocks and the Three Bears. – In a m-n-te!

Antworten:

6

1. She's four years older than Adam.
2. He felt excited, scared and a little bit proud. He really wanted to go to school.
3. Because his school uniform was red.

8

1. Because it was his first day at school.
2. No, he wasn't happy. He didn't want his mum to leave.
3. Because he didn't like him.

10

1. She went into the forest to find some breakfast.
2. No, they weren't; they were out.
3. No, he didn't want to eat her. He wanted to play with her.

12

1. Father Bear was the biggest.
2. He looked quite cute.
3. The most dangerous thing she did was to go to sleep on Baby Bear's bed.

14

1. It was called the school hall.
2. You decide.

16

1. You decide.
2. You decide.

up	down
never	always
bad	good
the same	different
out	in
stop	go
quiet	noisy
easy	difficult
cute	scary
safe	dangerous
go to sleep	wake up

Adam is almost five. He's very young, but he's a polite child. He always says thank you.

My dad says English is quite easy. But I'm terrible at it!

Your English is better than my English.

Please read me the story of Goldilocks and the Three Bears. – In a minute!

Vielen Dank, dass Sie diese Reihe gelesen haben.

Wenn Sie Fragen oder Vorschläge zur Verbesserung des Buches haben, schicken Sie mir bitte eine E-Mail an: lydiawinter.zigzagenglish@gmail.com. Vorschläge für neue Bücher sind auch immer willkommen.

Die Website finden Sie hier: **www.zigzagenglish.co.uk**. Auf dieser Website können Sie und Ihr Kind sich über unsere anderen Bücher für Kinder und Erwachsene informieren und unseren Blog lesen. Sie finden dort auch weitere englischsprachige Aktivitäten.

Ich würde mich freuen, wenn Sie eine Buchrezension hinterlassen. Vielen Dank!

Hier sind einige Auszüge aus unseren anderen Büchern für Kinder, die anfangen, Englisch zu lernen:

From: I Speak English Too! - 1

10B  

Sam: Do you like **shopping**, Jack?

Jack: Yes, I love shopping. I like **buying** new **clothes** with my mum.

Sam: **How often** do you buy new clothes?

Jack: Quite often. Maybe **once a month**.

Sam: I like new clothes too. But my mum says they're too **expensive**.

Jack: Some clothes shops are **cheap**. And buying online is cheap too.

Sam: I really want some new **trainers**. But the ones I like are very expensive.

Jack: Maybe **wait** till **Christmas**?

Sam: What do you want for Christmas?

Jack: I want a new **jacke**t. A beautiful red one. It's online.

Sam: Is it cheap?

Jack: No, not really. But it's for Christmas!

From: I Speak English Too! - 2

8A: A week's holiday

Katie: It's my **half term** holiday next week. A **whole** week with no school!

Anna: Are you going **away**?

Katie: Yes. We're going to the Lake District.

Anna: What's that? Where is it?

Katie: It's in the **north** of England. There are lots of **mountains** and **lakes**. It's very beautiful.

Anna: Lucky you! I have school next week.

Katie: School is really hard at the moment. I'm tired. I need a **break**.

Anna: Is your whole family going?

Katie: No. My mum has to work next week. So she's **staying** at home.

Anna: Your **poor** mum.

From: Read English with Ben - 1

14. Present

The day after the last day of school was the first day of the summer holidays. But Ben didn't feel excited. He felt unhappy.

He **lay** on his bed in his bedroom with a book. But he didn't read the book. He thought about all those years at primary school. He thought about his friends.

His mum **called** him. "It's lunchtime, Ben! Come downstairs!"

Ben **sighed**. He went downstairs to the dining room. He **started** to say: "I'm not hungry, mum. I don't want any lunch." But then he stopped. What was that on the table? It was a **parcel.** Was it a **present**? For him?

From: The Learn English Activity Book for Children

CATEGORIES

WRITE DOWN 3:

1. School subjects
2. Small pets
3. Nice things to eat
4. Languages
5. Books in English
6. Annoying things children in your class do
7. Sea animals
8. English songs
9. Plants
10. Horrible things to eat
11. Funny people
12. Nice things to do on holiday
13. Jobs you don't want to do when you grow up
14. Long English words
15. Sports
16. Vegetables
17. Things your parents can do that you can't do
18. Short English words
19. Countries
20. American movies

Which Zigzag book is this picture from? Can you colour it in?

www.ingramcontent.com/pod-product-compliance
Lightning Source LLC
LaVergne TN
LVHW010104110826
845155LV00028B/475

* 9 7 8 1 9 1 4 9 1 1 6 3 7 *